THE GATHERING OF THE KOALAS AT MEREDITH

Rolf Schlagloth; Flavia Santamaria & Gayle Newcombe

Copyright © 2019 Rolf Schlagloth; Flavia Santamaria.

All rights reserved. No part of this book may be used or reproduced by any means, graphic, electronic, or mechanical, including photocopying, recording, taping or by any information storage retrieval system without the written permission of the author except in the case of brief quotations embodied in critical articles and reviews.

Balboa Press books may be ordered through booksellers or by contacting:

Balboa Press
A Division of Hay House
1663 Liberty Drive
Bloomington, IN 47403
www.balboapress.com.au
1 (877) 407-4847

Because of the dynamic nature of the Internet, any web addresses or links contained in this book may have changed since publication and may no longer be valid. The views expressed in this work are solely those of the author and do not necessarily reflect the views of the publisher, and the publisher hereby disclaims any responsibility for them.

Any people depicted in stock imagery provided by Getty Images are models, and such images are being used for illustrative purposes only.
Certain stock imagery © Getty Images.

Interior Image Credit: Gayle Newcombe

ISBN: 978-1-5043-1889-1 (sc)
ISBN: 978-1-5043-1890-7 (e)

Print information available on the last page.

Balboa Press rev. date: 09/05/2019

The Gathering of the Koalas at Meredith

Text: Rolf Schlagloth & Flavia Santamaria
Artwork & illustrations: Gayle Newcombe

Rolf and Flavia dedicate this book to their children Ludovica, Alessia, Riccardo and Anneliese. May they be the leaders of a brighter natural future.

Foreword

Every living species is like a precious, irreplaceable work of art … unique and beyond price. Each living thing represents millions of years of continuous adaptation and evolution to suit the ever-changing planetary environment. All living species are but single beats of the giant heart we humans call Mother Earth. Her biosphere gifts freely to us everything we need for sustained life. But, miss a single beat, and that giant heart of nature begins to falter.

As a keystone species in many Australian ecosystems the koala's fate is inextricably linked to the ongoing health of the bushland where it chooses to live. Anything that harms the koala in turn harms the bush and those ongoing ripples affect us all. By contrast of course, anything that helps a living species to live in balance with its habitat by turn does us good also.

Rolf Schlagloth and Flavia Santamaria are two passionately dedicated koala biologists and environmental educators. Both have worked tirelessly for decades to raise awareness of the ongoing plight of koalas and their associated habitats. In writing this valuable and much needed book, they have shone a clear, bright light on that powerful flagship species for conservation … the magnificent Australian koala. This book is an effective tool for understanding; showing us we need to look twice at our world … with both the head and the heart.

Foreword cont.

The very clear message of their delightful book is to cherish and nurture the wonderfully complex environment which supports all beings but even more importantly, to hold our own selves accountable, since everything we do or choose not to do, has ongoing impacts on the other lifeforms with whom we share this planet.

As a professional wildlife and conservation artist, I recognised, long ago, the value of words and art to capture the minds of both children and adults. In bringing true environmental understanding to people, it is crucial to first engage their hearts. Once you have their hearts the minds will naturally want to follow.

Teamed with Gayle Newcombe's delightful illustrations, Rolf and Flavia take us all on a much-needed journey with the inspiring young koala who learns to listen with her heart to the world around her and chooses to make positive changes. This is something we all need to do.

Steve Morvell
www.stevemorvell.com
https://www.facebook.com/steve.morvell

The Gathering of the Koalas at Meredith

Big Old Manna Gum, in the paddock near Meredith, showed her age. She bore many hollows and some thick branches, albeit fewer and fewer leaves after years of drought and degradation of the surrounding land.

She had been there for a long time before farming even started and before trees around her were cut down for firewood and gold mining.

“People only listen to reports on economic growth, but not to the lamenting of nature”, she moaned.

Her small branches were waving a sad hello towards the few surrounding weakened snow gums and swamp gums that had been spared from clearing. The ground between these trees was dry and only weeds grew there; tree saplings never making it to maturity, hungry stock eating anything fresh.

Full of thoughts and sorrow, she hid her soul into the hollow in her massive trunk. There, in the depth of the nothingness, she evolved the idea—a future for the trees, a future for the koalas. A future for all.

“We can’t wait any longer, we need to act now!” she cried. “I am inviting all the influential koalas for a consultation on collaborative action.”

And they came by the thousands, carrying statutes, rules and legislations. Ready to protect the environment, all expenses paid by their government departments, NGOs and industry groups.

Big Old Manna Gum saw the tide of koalas approaching. Are they ready to listen? Is this a new beginning? Was there hope? She wondered. One by one, they were climbing hastily on her branches.

They arrived with securely locked briefcases. Those who had been awarded scientific medals were flashing them on their chest. Politicians and ministers were identifiable by their grimaces. Those who were known to be swinging voters could be identified by their gait, and those coming from industry stood out by a mile. Some were still hiding their awards and intentions from others.

The Big Old Manna Gum filled up rapidly and so they soon were able to start a plenary session.

She welcomed all participants in the name of all things living, including humans.

One by one, the honourable members presented their cases; first up, the scientists.

The ecologist began, "I want to stress the need for using a systematic root cause analysis and promote a quantifying investigation."

The geologist added, "May I link the drop in water table in some areas to short sighted mining activities?" and the representative from the Environment Protection Authority responded. "We noticed high levels of air pollution near unrestrained mineral processing projects."

The senior forecaster from the weather bureau used past records to explain current climatic challenges and modelled future scenarios that were frightening to all stakeholders.

The microbiologist claimed, "Changes in temperatures have already affected enzyme activities across all strata." And the chemist contributed, "I have witnessed reduced water availability and changes to nutrients in leaves."

The presentations were spiked with scientific language and foreign sounding words. The audience were quiet, as if they were observing a moment of silence during a memorial service; if they were not overwhelmed by the seriousness of the language, they felt the gravity of the scenario depicted by the scientists.

The echoing of the concerns didn't abate.

The historians went back in time, "Please, let's not forget how Indigenous Australians were able to live for thousands of years with koalas and their habitat in a sustainable way, and how the arrival of the Europeans dramatically reduced the eucalypt forest and has driven the koala to near extinction in just over two-hundred years."

The ecologists and foresters stressed, “Trees are not only important for us koalas, but for life in general as they absorb CO_2 and release oxygen which life on Earth needs for breathing. Trees actually communicate with each other and removing vegetation from within a forest can have detrimental effects on the individual trees as well as on the whole ecosystem.”

Some were suggesting solutions. The organic farmer asserted, “I discourage the use of chemicals and promote the keeping of trees as windbreaks and nature refuges.” Meanwhile a representative from the clergy revealed that the doctrine had been changed to reflect that no divine intervention is to be expected to solve the human-made issue.

Questions were arising. “Why haven’t we learnt from past mistakes? We introduced pest species like foxes, rabbits, cane toads, gorse, lantana and prickly pear, many of which compete with, often out-compete, injure or predate upon our native species including us,” the life-scientist pointed out.

The audience became impatient, some were overwhelmed by the litany of complaints about past mistakes causing the current disastrous situation, while others wanted to see some quick action.

A statistician got the word, and numbers were flying around like protons in a large Hadron Collider, creating more confusion without ever reaching the target.

The psychologist, was arguing that nature calms us down. He was attempting to convince them that the green of the leaves, and the other bright colours exhibited by many flowers, were nature’s gift to us to keep us sane; it didn’t instil tranquillity to the crowd.

A very wealthy entrepreneur was suggesting to use a private-public model to advance his well-progressed prototype space plane to start “ferrying people to other planets before Earth is damaged to the point of no-repair.” “So to stuff up the other planets as well?” an older member bellowed from the worried crowd. “What else can we do?” another member shouted.

The mob became very alarmed and unsettled. Suddenly all went silent; a politician had made his way to the highest branch.

He was an imposing personality. Appearing convincing, strong and stylish. His gestures were well rehearsed, they were those of a well-seasoned politician with media training and acting coaching. His performance reminiscent of great orators from the past, many of whom, unfortunately, were later exposed to have harboured evil intentions.

His speech attracted the attention of all. He welcomed the traditional owners of the land, highlighted the importance of all present, and made each koala, and the Big Old Manna Gum feel important and special. “As I am speaking, new technologies are being discovered which, under my leadership, will counter any of the threats that are being publicised and blown out of proportion today.” He elaborated that, under his government, the country had installed the largest ever research and education budget which would soon kick in and assist in remediating most of these past slipups. The funding awarded to gene research projects would enable the development of trees that could use higher atmospheric concentrations of CO_2 and withstand the projected frequent and more severe droughts and the one-in-a-hundred year flood events anticipated to happen every five years. “The sky is the limit and my government is taking us there.”

Relieved, representatives from industry groups applauded the loudest and shouted “We have been saying for some time that all the concerns are part of a total overreaction—let’s come back in another year, wait and see and not waste money and energy.” Many koalas relaxed and were ready to put all actions on hold.

Suddenly, a koala who recently was conferred the ‘Young Koala of the Year’, but had held back so far during the proceedings, emerged from the crowd.

“We have totally missed the aim of this gathering here.” Despite her smaller stature, her passion made her appear taller than all of them.

“We can’t just remain spectators, we need to act and we need to act now.” The young koala was waving her arms around and her gestures demanded attention.

“Non-action will take us to a point of no-return, we need to participate in a process of change and encourage the public to engage in this process. Koalas are a flagship species and, as such, we need to lead this change and not become the canary in the mineshaft.”

“We can’t just continue with business as usual. There is still time to change things and reduce the overall impact while at the same time adapting to new conditions. We need direct action and we need it now.”

Big Old Manna Gum was crying tears of joy and gratitude, and congratulated the little koala. “Finally, someone who speaks from the heart and is not just looking for excuses.”

However, her joy didn't last long.

"But what can we do? We are only individuals with few resources and little influence." The expressions of doubt quickly returned to all. More questions were raised and the previously experienced uncertainty and disarray returned. When doubtful exclamations by the crowd threatened to escalate into chaos, the politicians and industry stakeholders salvaged the moment, took the opportunity and quickly recaptured the meeting. Eventually the meeting was closed, like every previous one, with a commitment to hold another one in the future.

Contentment re-established, trust instilled that the politicians and their industry partners would make the necessary changes without any significant impact on the economy or inconvenience to everyone's lifestyle. Participants departed joyous, jokes were made, hands were shaken and gifts exchanged, all while dressed up in colourful garments - like they had done so many times before.

The media obtained their interviews and briefings full of carefully crafted one-liners and promises; while not noticing that there was no long-lasting concept behind the clouds of pretence.

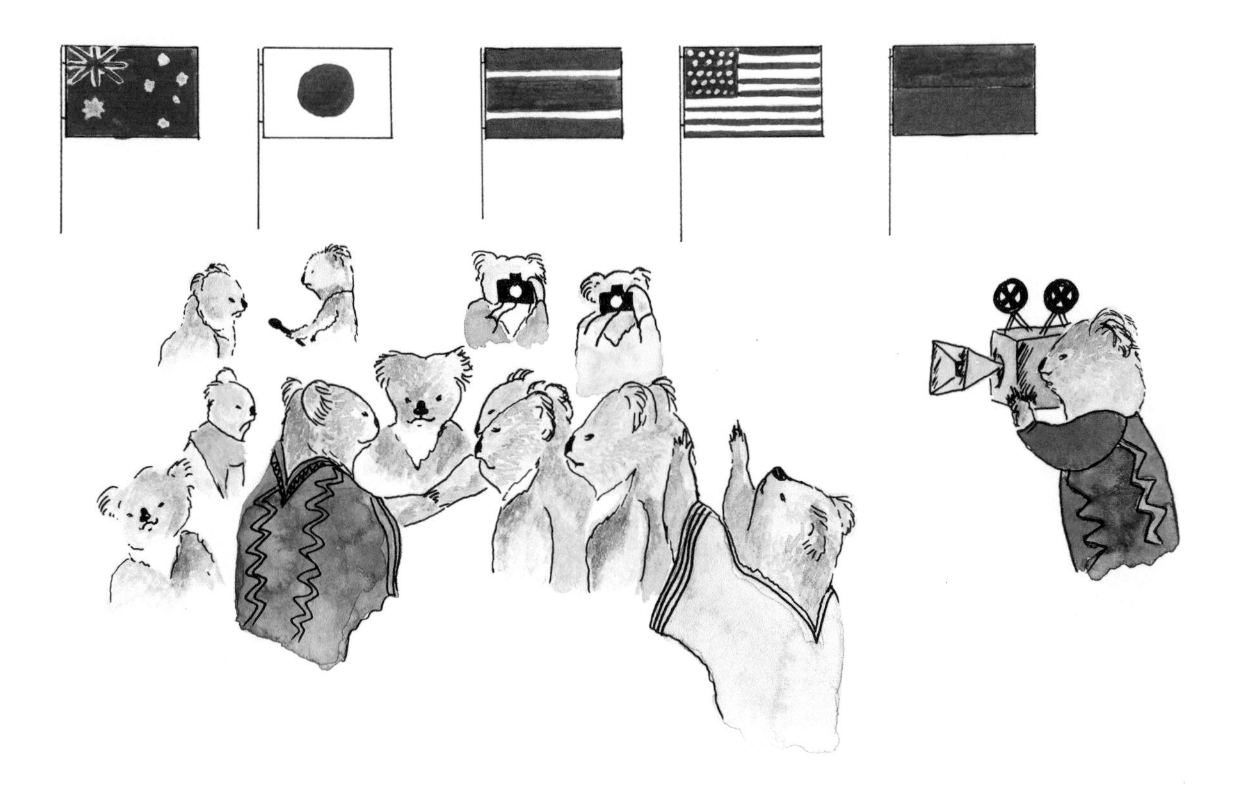

Eventually silence returned. Big Old Manna Gum was tired, her few leaves hanging lifelessly from a few spindly branches. Night was approaching fast with a sandstorm in the distance picking up plenty of dry plant material and many plastic bags, bottles and food wraps discarded by thoughtless people.

At the base of her trunk was the young koala, curled up and lifeless. The only one who had spoken from her heart, the only one with a spirit, seemed to be dead.

Just before daybreak, the young koala rose and meandered in the direction of the rising sun, although today, the dark grey clouds only allowed a glimmer of light to shine through.

For days she walked past dry rivers and defoliated trees. A landscape devoid of life, awful smells that discouraged her from resting even for a minute.

Eventually she arrived at what, from a distance, appeared to be a lake. On its shores were stalls, where koalas were selling plastic eucalypt trees that had been showered in eucalyptus oils, bottles containing drinking-water that was brown like soil, and foods that had obviously been exposed to stagnant waters. She could see dead fish floating in the brackish lake devoid of any oxygen. Most of the infrequent fresh water was diverted further upstream to satisfy the rich and powerful who owned the factories making plastics.

Stalls were surrounded by see-through plastic tarps and air was pumped through by huge conditioners that frequently added air freshener of various scents. All this was accompanied by classical music by Wagner, giving it an eerie feeling. Only the very rich could afford to buy anything and they were escorted by private security at all times. Solar-powered machines drove around dispersing odourising eucalyptus or lavender pellets to compensate for the terribly bad smells. The rich were recovering from their exhausting shopping trip by lazing at the edge of the lake in their bright red banana lounges. The koala was disgusted and disappointed. She had hoped that her escape would have taken her to a brighter and better world.

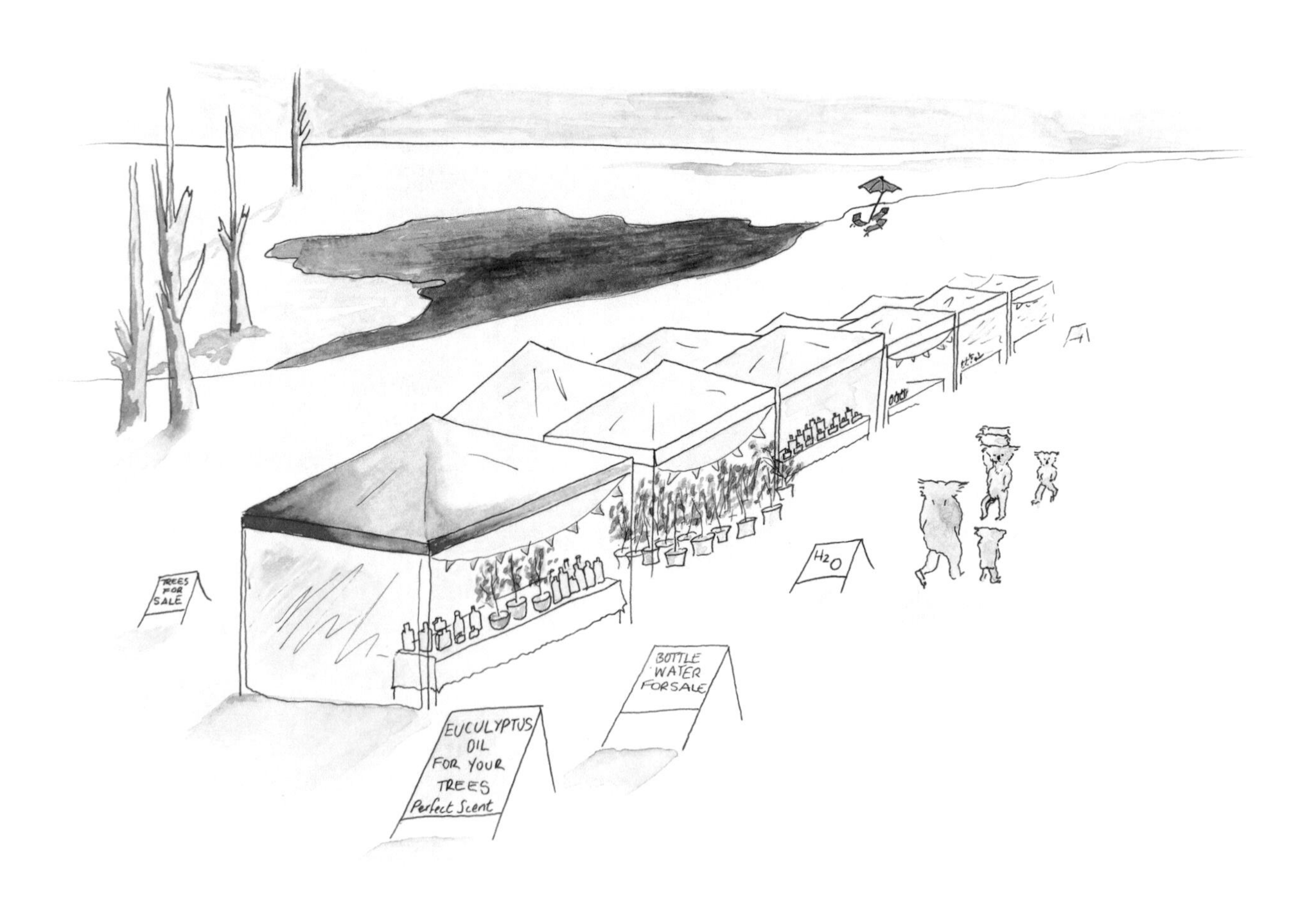

Sad and in deep resignation, she walked past an avenue of trees unable to distinguish the plastic from the dead ones.

Hungry, tired and extremely disenchanted she sat down in the middle of nowhere and fell asleep.

She dreamed about how she and her fellow beings had been thinking too much of themselves, looked far too deep into issues and waited for complex and far-reaching solutions. Images of the devastated landscapes and dead trees passed by her like scenes in a movie.

The image of her grandfather appeared to her. A wise, old male koala spoke to her from behind, whispering in her ear. It felt like a game of Secret Whispers, he was gently reminding her of the fun they had playing in the eucalypt forests when all was still wonderful. When they were swinging on the small but leafy branches to see who could climb furthest out in the canopy and nibble on the juiciest of young leaves. They had to trust their judgement when attempting to climb those small branches—a judgement based on personal experiences, on observations she made of her parents and siblings.

Her grandfather reminded her of the highly refined senses that koalas possess. A heightened sense of smell that can detect nutrients and poison in individual leaves and a very fine-tuned hearing to detect any sound of danger or a cracking noise in a branch.

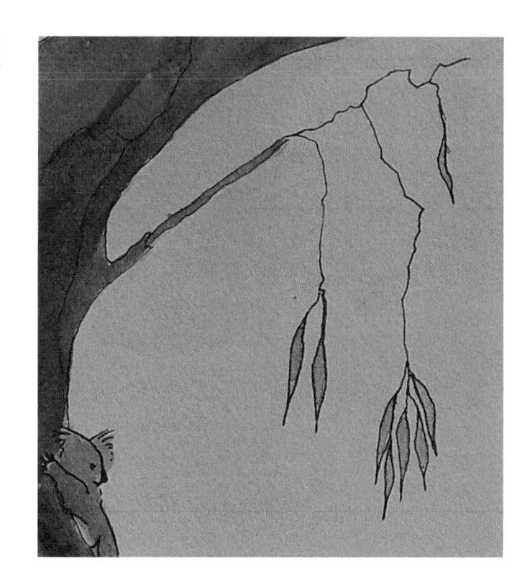

“Use these senses to make informed decisions and find simple but effective solutions,” he softly spoke to her.

She replied to her grandfather, “It is so nice to see you again, thank you so much for your counsel.” He didn’t respond, he had left as he did many years earlier when he was a young male. As all male koalas, he left to establish his home-range, away from his parents. But she, Big Old Manna Gum, was still there—was it all a dream?

Big Old Manna Gum appeared smiling at her.

She woke up and returned to the place where it all started, leaving behind the deserted and bleak landscape.

A new awakening.

She was now ready to face all life lessons given to her. With bated breath, she approached Big Old Manna Gum and saw, to her surprise, that a new sapling was growing beneath her majestic canopy.

The young koala was ready to receive her instructions.

"Enable life to flourish, protect native vegetation and replant where it has been lost! Be a servant to nature at all times!"

For the sapling was born from silence, not noise.

Suggested reading:

Dickens, R. K. (1975)**.** The koala (*Phascolarctos cinereus*) past, present and future. *Australian Veterinary Journal*, 51(10), 459-463.

Martin, R., & Handasyde, K. A. (1999). *The koala: natural history, conservation and management*. UNSW press.

Menkhorst, P. (2008). *Hunted, marooned, re-introduced, contracepted: a history of Koala management in Victoria.* Too Close for Comfort: Contentious Issues in Human–Wildlife Encounters' (Eds D. Lunney, A. Munn and W. Meikle.) pp, 73-92.

Phillips, B. (1990). *Koalas: the little Australians we'd all hate to lose.* Australian Government Pub Service.

Santamaria, F., & Schlagloth, R. (2016). The effect of *Chlamydia* on translocated *Chlamydia*-naïve koalas: a case study. *Australian Zoologist*, 38(2), 192-202.

Santamaria, F., Keatley, M., & Schlagloth, R. (2005). Does size matter? Tree use by translocated koalas. *The Victorian Naturalist*, 122(1), 4–12.

Schlagloth, R., Santamaria, F., Golding, B., & Thomson, H. (2018). Why is it important to Use Flagship Species in Community Education? The Koala as a Case Study. *Animal Studies Journal*, 7(1), 127-148.

Schlagloth, R., Cahir, F., & Clark, I. (2018). The Importance of the Koala in Aboriginal Society in Nineteenth-century Victoria (Australia): A Reconsideration of the Archival Record. *Anthrozoös*, 31(4), 433-441.

Wedrowicz, F., Wright, W., Schlagloth, R., Santamaria, F., & Cahir, F. (2017). Landscape, koalas and people: A historical account of koala populations and their environment in South Gippsland. *Australian Zoologist*, 38(4), 518-536.

Wohlleben, P. (2016). *The Hidden Life of Trees: What They Feel, How They Communicate—Discoveries from A Secret World.* Black Inc.

Inspiration for this book

Rolf Schlagloth & Flavia Santamaria are both koala researchers and educators who believe in the power of the koala as a flagship species for changing the world into a better, healthier place with a thriving environment for all flora and fauna. A place where we, humans and other species, can live in harmony with our surroundings without destroying our own living space and that of others.

The Big Old Manna Gum lives in a paddock near Meredith in the state of Victoria; she is indeed a real Manna Gum (*Eucalyptus viminalis*), home to a number of koalas who were part of a research project that investigated the diet and movement of these animals under threat from cars and loss of habitat (trees). Manna gums are one of the preferred fodder species for koalas in Victoria and remnant stands are often under threat from development and suffer from lack of regrowth in agricultural landscapes.

Rolf & Flavia have witnessed, for several decades now, how we humans continue to ignore the threats to the long-term survival of our koalas and the health of our environment in general. The plot of this book is heavily influenced by the experiences they had with the animals and plants they encountered, but also by the political games they have witnessed being played with the health of our planet. While this is a book of fiction, many scenes reflect situations we are currently experiencing around Australia, e.g. Murray Darling Basin water stress, plastic recycling crisis. The authors hope that you, the reader, were able to identify a few scenes that stimulate discussion and reflection.

This story was inspired by this remnant *Eucalyptus* tree, in the paddock near Meredith.

'There is no place like home' (koala mother & daughter)
by illustrator and wildlife artist Gayle Newcombe.
For greeting cards of this drawing and other beautiful
originals and commissions, please visit:
https://www.facebook.com/gaylenewcombefineart/ or email Gayle at:
countrycolours224@gmail.com

Printed in the United States
By Bookmasters